Platypus

DISCOVER

Platypus

There is only one species of the Platypus. It is a monotreme. This is a mammal that lays eggs instead of giving birth to its young live. The Platypus is an odd looking animal, which you will discover in greater detail later on. In fact, in this book we are going to discover all sorts of cool facts about Platypus, like where it can be found, its extraordinary abilities and much more. Read on to be totally amazed with this strange creature.

Where in the World?

Did you know the Platypus can be found in Eastern Australia, including Tasmania? This creature likes to hang out in freshwater lakes and streams. When it is out of the water it likes to spend time on the banks of the river or under a gathering of tree roots.

The Body of a Platypus

Did you know this creature has the bill of a duck, the tail of beaver and the feet of an otter? The male platypus is bigger than the female. He can measure from 20 inches (50 centimeters) in total length. The females are around 17 inches long (43 centimeters). The Platypus can weigh up to 5.3 pounds (2.4 kilograms).

The Fur of a Platypus

Did you know this animal has fine dense fur? In fact, there are about eight hundred hairs per square millimeter. It also has two layers of hair; a woolly undercoat and long guard fur on top. These two layers trap air and keep the platypus from drying out. Its hair is also waterproof.

Platypus Tail

Did you know the flat tail of the Platypus is very cool? Its tail is used as a stabiliser during swimming and allows it to dive very quickly. The tail is covered in coarse hairs. During the winter months, when food is scarce, it can live on the fat stores in its tail.

Platypus Bill

Did you know the platypus has a large leathery bill? If you were to touch the bill of this animal it would feel soft and rubbery. The top of the bill is a blue-grey in colour. Just slightly back from its tip are the Platypus's two nostril holes. With the nostrils being here, it allows this animal to rest in the water with just its eyes peeking out.

The Platypus Feet

AMNH/ R. Mickens

Did you know this animal has short legs with clawed feet? The front feet of the Platypus are webbed. This makes it a great swimmer. The back feet are only partially webbed. These act as steering rudders when the animal is underwater. The platypus is quite mobile on land, but carries itself on its knuckles.

The Platypus Poison

Did you know the Platypus is venomous? Only the males are venomous. He has a long sharp spur (like a claw) on the ankles of his hind feet. This spur is connected to a gland where the poison comes from. This can cause great pain to humans. But mostly the platypus uses this to defend himself against other males.

What a Platypus Eats

Did you know this animal is a carnivore? That means it likes to eat mostly meat. The platypus will dine on worms, insect larvae, shrimp and crayfish. It can eat up to 20 percent of its total body weight in one day. The platypus does not eat with its bill. Its mouth is located under its bill.

The Platypuses Special Ability

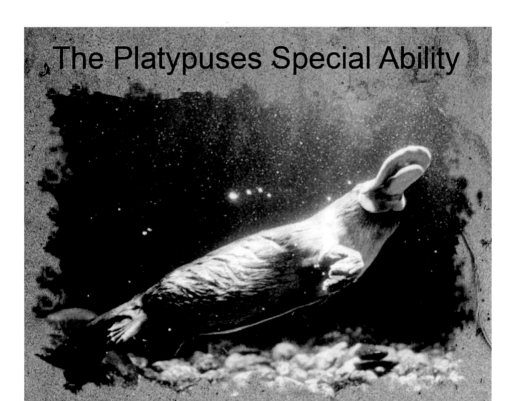

Did you know the Platypus uses electroreception to find its prey? This means it can sense the electrical impulses being given off by other creatures. The platypus sticks its bill into the sand. From here it can sense when a tasty snack is nearby. After it catches its food, this animal stuffs it into its large cheek pouches, then returns to the surface to eat it.

The Platypus Burrow

Did you know this animal makes a burrow just above the water level? Its burrow has an oval section. It may also have two ends of entry or exit. This burrow can be up to 98 feet long (30 metres). If the female feels threatened, she may extend the length of the burrow to keep her young safe.

Platypus Mom and Dad

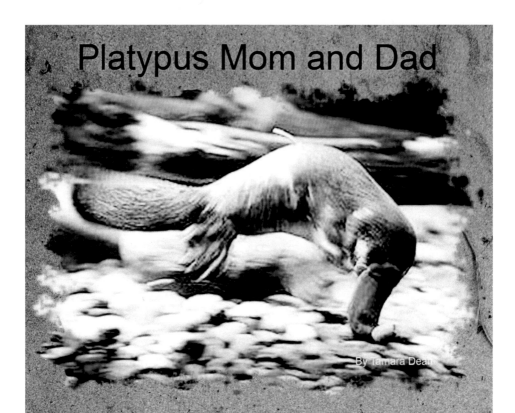

By Tamara Dean

Did you know the male platypus uses its toxic spurs to fight for a female? After the male has won the female's favor they will mate. This is between June and October. She will carry her eggs for about a month. After she lays them she will curl around them for about 10 days. Then they will hatch.

The Baby Platypus

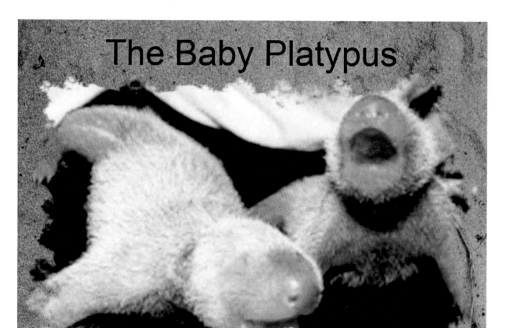

Did you know the platypus eggs are soft like lizard eggs? Newborn platypuses are born blind, hairless and helpless. Unlike most creatures that hatch out of eggs, the babies of the platypus suckle milk from their mother. The babies feed on the milk for 3 to 4 months.

Predators of the Platypus

By Stefan Kraft

Did you know this animal has many natural predators? Depending on where they live, this animal can be hunted by snakes, water rats, goannas, hawks, owls, and eagles. The platypus in Australia are often taken by crocodiles. Men once hunted this animal; however, it is now protected.

The Platypus and People

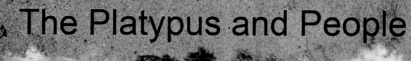

Did you know the platypus is not endangered? However, pollution levels in its natural habitat are causing harm to this weird animal. Deforestation is also causing the platypus to lose its natural home. If you would like to see a platypus up close, there are many zoos that have these wonderful creatures.

Life of a Platypus

Did you know the platypus in the wild can live over 10 years? They spend most of the day resting in their burrows. They will also spend time hunting for food and basking in the sun. This animal also enjoys grooming its dense fur out in the open.

Quiz

Question 1: The Platypus is a monotreme, what does that mean?

Answer 1: It is a mammal that lays eggs instead of giving birth live

Question 2: What does the Platypus tail look like?

Answer 2: It is flat with coarse hair on it.

Question 3: Where does the venom come from on a male platypus?

Answer 3: The spurs found on the ankles of its back feet

Question 4: How does the Platypus sense its food?

Answer 4: With electrical impulses called, *electroreception*

Question 5: What is the lifespan of a wild platypus?

Answer 5: Over 10 years

Thank you for checking out another title from DISCOVER Books! Make sure to check out Amazon.com for many other great books.

Made in United States
North Haven, CT
08 February 2024

48523330R00018